Let's Get Ready to Move!

Written and Illustrated by

Beth Breaux

To Isabel

My name is June! And I have some news.
My family is selling our house...

and moving to a new house on a new road in a new town.

The new house will look a little bit different
than the house we live in now.

But it will still have a kitchen, a living room, a bathroom
... and even a bedroom for me!

"But what about all the cups and the plates and my rocking horse? What about all the books and our clothes... and my teddy!?" I ask.

"The dishes will miss us.

Who will rock on the horse?

Why can't all those books come with us, too?"

"They can! Before we go to our new house on a new road in a new town, we will pack all those things in boxes...

and just to make extra special sure we don't leave anything behind, you can help us!" Mommy says.

Mommy makes sure the dishes are wrapped up carefully before adding them to the boxes.

"All done with the dishes, June!" she says.

"Make sure to wrap my rocking horse carefully, too!"

We add the horse to a box. I can't wait
to rock on her at the new house on a new road
in a new town.

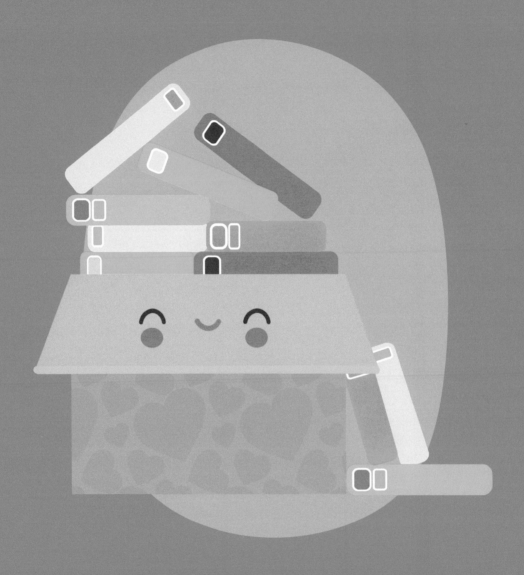

Next, we pack all our books. There sure are a lot!

And then we pack all our clothes. Some of Mommy and
Daddy's clothes can stay on a clothes rail. All my clothes
fit in two boxes. Even my winter coat and
all my pajamas are coming to the
new house on a new road in a new town.

We pack all my toys last of all so I can play with them up until the very last second.

Now that my toys are all packed, I'm getting excited to go.
But wait...

"Don't forget Teddy!" I squeal.

Daddy says, "Teddy can ride with us
in the car! We won't put him
in any of the boxes."

Everything is packed and
ready to go!

So many boxes!

Daddy uses a hand cart to bring all our boxes
outside and load them on the moving truck.
He is so strong!

Even our furniture goes in the truck.

The truck driver will drive all our things to the new town... to the new road...

We won't say goodbye to our dishes and clothes.

We won't say farewell to my rocking horse and books.

We will say, "See you later!"

Because all our things will meet us there.

Daddy will unload all our furniture and boxes.
And I will unpack all my toys.

The house may be a little messy for a while. We must figure out where everything goes.

But in the meantime,
I can have fun playing in all the boxes!

"Your new room will look a lot like your old room.
Your books will be there.
Your toys will be there.
Rocking horse will be ready for rocking and Teddy will be ready for snuggling." Mommy says.

"In fact, there's a lot that will be the same about the new house on the new road in the new town. Most important of all is that Mommy and Daddy will be there..."

"...and I'll be there, too!" I say.

"Yes, you'll be there too," Mommy giggles. "We will all be together just like in the old house. And our love can fill up any home."

27738306R00019